OUR MUTTS

By Patrick McDonnell

**Andrews McMeel
Publishing**

Kansas City

Other Books by Patrick McDonnell

Mutts
Cats and Dogs: Mutts II
More Shtuff: Mutts III
Yesh!: Mutts IV

Mutts Sundays
The Mutts Little Big Book

Mutts is distributed internationally by King Features Syndicate, Inc. For information write King Features Syndicate, Inc., 235 East 45th Street, New York, New York 10017.

01 02 03 04 BAH 10 9 8 7 6 5 4 3

ISBN: 0-7407-0456-7

Library of Congress Catalog Card Number: 00-103478

Our Mutts is printed on recycled paper.

AHH... JANUARY FIRST.. TIME TO TURN OVER A **NEW LEAF.**

Z

OH, GREAT SHPHINX, WHAT DOES THE FUTURE HOLD IN THE NEW MILLENNIUM**?**

FISH WILL SHWIM... BIRDS WILL FLY... **CATS** WILL **RULE** THE **WORLD.**

HMMM... NOTHIN' NEW

SHTATUS QUO.

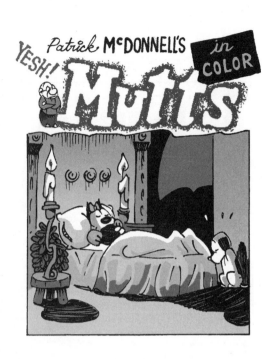

9

MEANWHILE BACK AT THE STARING CONTEST...

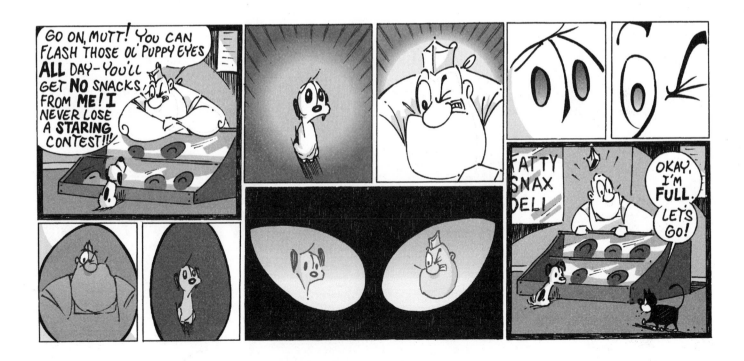

Page 25

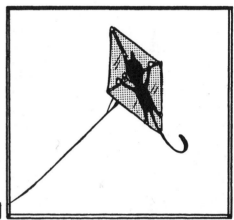

MUTTS

by

Patrick McDonnell

❁

MCMXCIX

Dame Millie felt a touch unstable.
Her little Mooch had set the table.

His Lady was even more surprised,
When Mooch himself carved the
chicky pot pie.

During dessert they gossiped
with glee,
As Mooch poured Millie
a cup of tea.

Then all was cleaned up,
and afterwards,
Earl joined in for a game of cards.

Mooch was usually so well
behaved,
Except he KNEW Earl
needed a shave.

When it got late Mooch stood
on his head,
And loudly declared He
would not go to bed!

But all good things must have
an end,
So Millie snored with her
furry friend.

As Frank says,
"WELL, THAT IS THAT."
His Dame Millie and her
Wonderful Cat.

EARL'S TEETH CLEANING WILL BE A SAFE, ROUTINE PROCEDURE.

THE ONLY PROBLEM I FORESEE IS WE MIGHT HAVE TO DO **ONE** EXTRACTION.

OH?

DOG FROM OWNER

EARL WILL BE FINE. WE'LL CALL YOU AFTER HIS TEETH CLEANING TO PICK HIM UP.

THERE, THERE.

I GUESS HE FOUND OUT **I** WAS THE ONE WHO ATE HIS SHOE.

EARL

HOWLWOOOO....

EARL'S TEETH CLEANING WENT **FINE**, BUT HE STILL MIGHT ACT A BIT **WOOZY** FROM THE ANESTHESIA.

C'MON, EARL, I KNOW YOU DIDN'T ENJOY YOUR TEETH CLEANING...

BUT A HEALTHY MOUTH LEADS TO A LONGER LIFE. YOU SHOULD BE GLAD

THAT'S BETTER

DR. WOO REMOVED **ALL MY TARTAR** AND OZZIE IS GO-ING TO BRUSH MY TEETH EVERY DAY!

SOUNDS LIKE A **LOT** OF WORK TO MAKE YOUR BREATH, SHWEET!

WHAT DO **YOU** RECOM-MEND?

FISH MINTS

34

MUDDAY...

DOOZDAY...

WHEN? DAY...

THIRDS DAY...

FLY DAY...

SCATTERDAY...

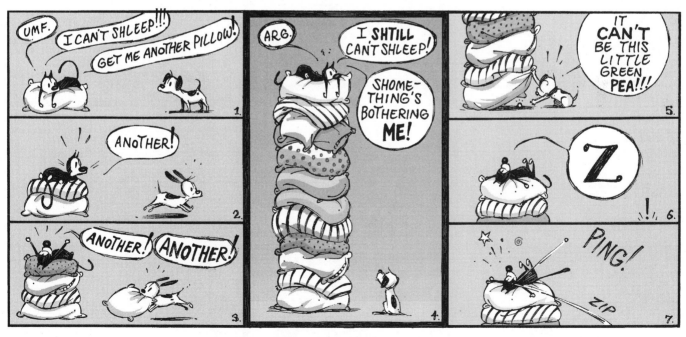

SHELTER STORIES "Tom-Tom"

THIS IS MY **BIG** CHANCE FOR ADOPTION. I'VE CLEANED MYSELF UP. NOW I JUST HAVE TO LOOK CUTE AND

THINK POSITIVE!

I'M A "KE
I'M A "KEE
I'M A "KEE

SHELTER STORIES "Tom-Tom"

ALL THESE PEOPLES! HOW WILL **I** KNOW WHICH IS THE RIGHT **ONE**!?!

ALL THESE KITTIES!!! HOW WILL **I** KNOW THE RIGHT **ONE**!?!

YOU'LL KNOW

THAT'S THE **ONE**!!!

SHELTER STORIES "Tom-Tom"

ANIMAL SHELTER

PET ADOPTATHON

IT'S **SO** WONDERFUL! WE'VE FOUND HOMES FOR THIRTY-ONE OF OUR ANIMALS...

NO!

32!

IS MASTER'S VOICE...

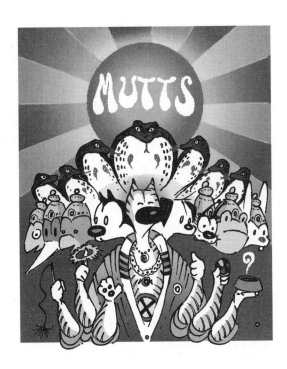

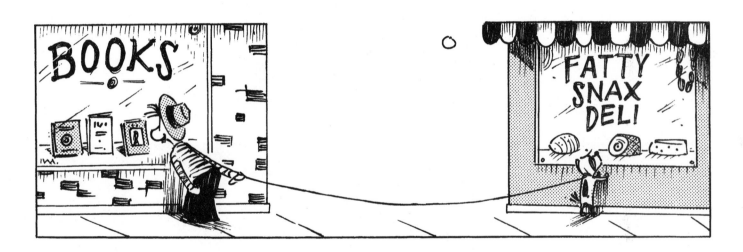

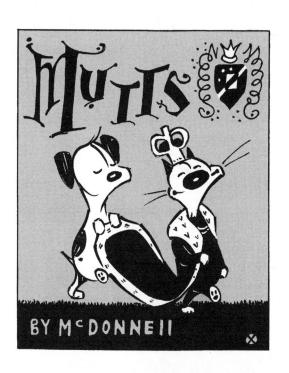

I'M **MOOCH**, THE **LION**, **KING** OF THE JUNGLE, **LORD** OF THE ANIMALS. MASHTER OF **ALL** HE...

... SHURVEYS.

HEY, MOOCH, WHAT'CHA DOIN'?

SHH... I'M A MIGHTY LION ON THE HUNT FOR ZEBRA

ZEBRA!?! THERE'S **NOT** A ZEBRA WITHIN A **THOUSAND** MILES FROM **HERE**!!!

NOT WITH ALL YOUR RACKET!!!

IN AN ATTEMPT TO **SHCARE** OUT SOME GAME THE MIGHTY LION **ROARS**...

MEOW!

HA·HA·HA·HA·HA

HYENAS.

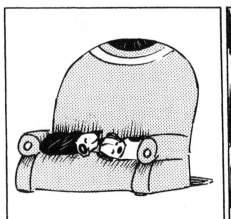

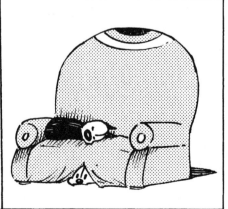

MUTTS

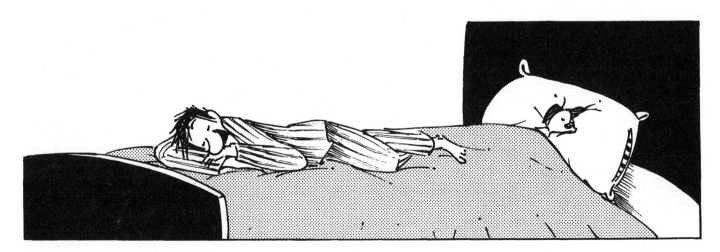

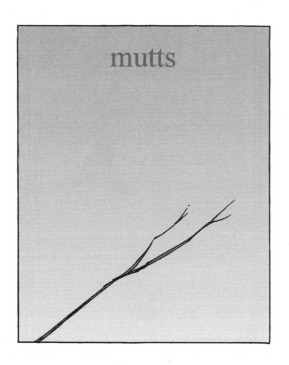

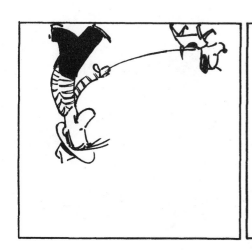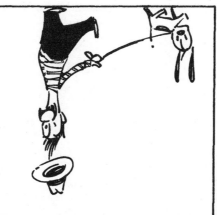

DINNER, DINNER, DINNER, DINNER, DINNER, DINNER, DINNER, DINNER, DINNER, DINNER, DINNER, DINNER

FWIP
FWIP
FWIP

DINNER, DINNER, DINNER, DINNER, DINNER, DINNER, DINNER, DINNER, DINNER, DINNER, DINNER, DINNER, DINNER

PUT ON THE AIR CONDITIONER

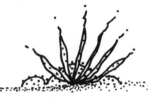

I NEED MY NAILS CLIPPED.

LET US KNOW WHEN IT'S **SAFE** TO FLY.

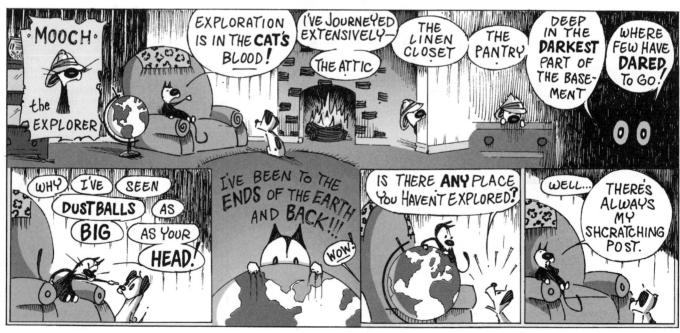

MOOCH, SHTINKY— DID YOU KNOW THERE'S A LIST OF "ENDANGERED" ANIMALS?

WHO!

ELEPHANTS, GORILLAS, OTTERS, PANDAS, BLACK RHINOS, SNOW LEOPARDS, EAGLES, TIGERS...

ARE LITTLE TABBY KITTIES WITH SLIGHTLY BIG NOSES ON **THAT** LIST!?!

EARL, WHAT MAKES A TIGER "ENDANGERED"?

IT'S WHEN A SPECIES IS "IN DANGER" OF BECOMING EXTINCT.

EXTINCT!

GONE FOREVER.

HOLD ME.

IF **BIG**, STRONG ANIMALS LIKE TIGERS AND ELFUNTS ARE ON THE ENDANGERED LIST...

HOW CAN A LITTLE GUY LIKE **ME** STAND A CHANCE!?! AAAAAUGH

I DON'T WANNA BE THE **LAST** OF THE SHTINKY PUDDIN'S!!!

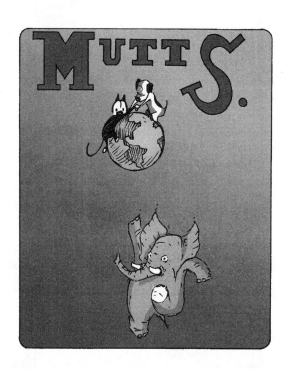

... RIGHT BEFORE OUR EYES...

HA!

SUPPER SURPRISE!

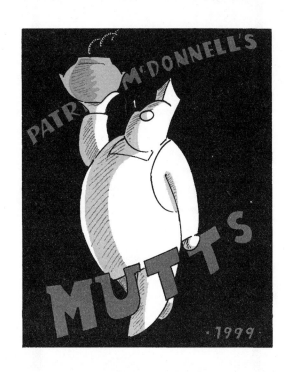

EVER SINCE EARL TOLD ME TIGERS ARE ENDANGERED, I FEEL LIKE I JUST CAN'T SIT AROUND AND DO **NOTHING!** IT'S **NOT** MY STYLE!!!

SO, YOU'LL GET **ALL** INVOLVED, GET **LOST** AND CAUSE A **BIG** COMMOTION.

I KNOW..

THAT'S MY STYLE.

EARL, MOOCH, I'VE DECIDED TO **SAVE** THE WORLD'S TIGERS.

YOU!?!

SOME-BODY HAS TO.

I WILL SAVE THE TIGERS

I WILL SAVE THE TIGERS.

I WILL SAVE THE TIGERS.

I WILL

I'M A **BIG** BELIEVER IN POSITIVE THINKING

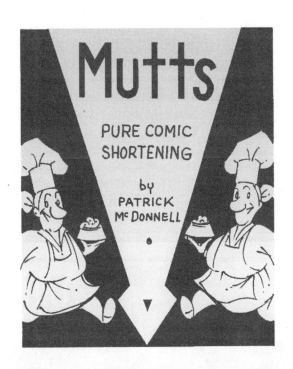

THE MUMMY

THE PHANTOM OF THE OPERA

SIT! STAY! STOP!

THE INCREDIBLE SHRINKING MAN

THE CREATURE FROM THE BLACK LAGOON

THE BLOB

THE INVISIBLE MAN

SHELTER STORIES ∘ "GRETCHEN"

THERE'S GRETCHEN. SHE'S BEEN CARING FOR ANIMALS FOR A LONG TIME.

IF SHE COULD— SHE WOULD TAKE US **ALL** HOME.

IF ONLY HER HOUSE WAS AS **BIG** AS HER HEART.

SHELTER STORIES ∘ "MARJORIE"

THAT'S MARJORIE! SHE LOGS IN MANY LONG HOURS AT THE SHELTER—BUT SHE ALWAYS HAS A SMILE.

SHE'S A **GOOD** ONE.

I'D ADOPT **HER.**

SHELTER STORIES ∘ "DR. WOO"

HERE'S DR. WOO, THE VET. SHE VOLUNTEERS AT THE SHELTER.

SHE SAYS "IT IS IN GIVING THAT WE RECEIVE."

... AND THAT'S THE BEST MEDICINE.

| SHELTER STORIES "RACHEL"  | AHH, RACHEL. SHE'S DEDICATED HER **WHOLE** LIFE TO HELP US. ... SO, SO MANY OF US. | SOMETIMES... I SEE HER CRY.  | I WISH I COULD HELP **HER**.  |

| SHELTER STORIES "TIDBIT"  | THE VOLUNTEERS HERE HAVE TAUGHT ME **SO** MUCH ABOUT DEVOTION, DEDICATION, COMPASSION AND LOVE.  | SIGH...  | NOW, I JUST NEED A **HOME** TO SHOW 'EM WHAT I LEARNED. |

| SHELTER STORIES "PAUL"  | THERE'S OFFICER PAUL! HE RESCUES ANIMALS...  | THE INJURED... THE ABUSED... THE LOST... THE ABANDONED...  | WE SALUTE YOU, OFFICER PAUL. |

MIRACLE ON 34th STREET...

THE YULE LOG...

THE NUTCRACKER...

CHRISTMAS TREE DECORATIONS...

UNDER THE MISTLETOE...

IT'S A WONDERFUL LIFE...

PURRRR...